Princess A.

Queen Victoria's Yoruba Godchild

First paperback printing, October 2019

U.K. version

ISBN: 978-0-9989007-7-3

Library of Congress Control Number: 2019913951

Copyright © 2019,
Wayne Goodman,
Ajuan Mance

waynegoodmanbooks

waynegoodmanbooks@gmail.com
Twitter: @WGoodmanbooks

Print versions at independent booksellers
Electronic versions on Kindle and Nook
Audiobooks from Audible and iTunes

Dedication

First, we must thank Aina, also known as Sarah Bonetta Forbes Davies, for her incredible life and the marvellous stories it has generated.

We also want to acknowledge our Readers who provided valuable feedback along the way: Richard May, Juanita Perryman, Gar McVey-Russell, Cass Sellars, Jill White, and Layla Wolfe.

Prelude

I wrote this book so that you, my friend, could read about the extraordinary, amazing life I have lived. Very few people get to experience what I have seen and heard.

As an adult, my role has been to teach young people like you. At the Female Institution at Sierra Leone, I got to share my experience and knowledge with others every day, and that has made me very happy.

And now, my friend, I can share my remarkable life with you. There are very few things I remember about my early years. The beginnings of my story come from what others have told me. Indeed, most of what I know about my own childhood came from the man who rescued me, Royal British Navy Captain Frederick E. Forbes.

–Aina Sarah Forbes Bonetta Davies

My Beginnings
Africa: Dahomey

Some time during the Yam Harvest of the 9883 *odun* (our Yoruba word for 'year'), I came into this world. My own mother and father named me Aina, but I do not remember much about them. The other tribeswomen told me my name meant the cord connecting me to my mother had wrapped around my neck when I was born.

Our family belonged to the Egbado clan of the Yoruba people. We lived in the village of Oke-Odan, which means "above the meadow" in your English-tongue. I cannot recall when the priest marked my face to show others that I was the daughter of the chief. They say I was just a baby when I received my markings, called *gombo*.

When I was in my fifth year, King Ghezo of Dahomey captured our family. He killed my parents and my siblings, but he did not kill me. He told me I was to be used for a special religious ceremony.

I remember King Ghezo's great palace of Dange-lah-cordeh in Abomey. Along the very high walls I could see old skulls. There were many tall huts and pavilions, but I lived in a small, dark barn with animals. The people who provided food called me, "Omoba." I told them my name was Aina, but they continued to say Omoba.

Without anyone I knew from my village, I felt very alone, and very scared. Some nights I would sing the songs I learned at home to comfort me until I finally fell asleep.

This was how my life was for many months. Back then, I did not yet have a grasp of how much time passed while I lay in captivity.

After a time unknown to me, perhaps a gloomy year or two, Captain Forbes arrived in Dahomey to speak with King Ghezo about trade matters. Before he got to meet with the King, the people of Dahomey celebrated with many days of feasts and parades. Each great man then presented gifts of greeting to the other.

During one of their meetings, King Ghezo displayed me to Captain Forbes. That was our first meeting. I had never seen such a pale person before. It seemed as if he had no skin at all. If he were a friend of King

Ghezo, he might have wanted to cause destruction and death as well. I could not look at his face because I feared his wrath.

The Captain looked down at me, put his hand beneath my chin and lifted it. He turned my head gently one way and then the other. When he spoke, his tongue sounded unfamiliar, and I could not understand his words.

Somehow, I feared my fate rested in the hand of this fearsome, pale man. King Ghezo had kept me in a dark place, but I felt that the mysterious Captain who spoke strangely might be my new conqueror. His unusual appearance frightened me, but I feared the King even more. He had killed the rest of my family, and I knew he had others killed with great swords.

King Ghezo told Captain Forbes I had been his prisoner for two years. I would be part of a special religious ritual to honour the King's ancestors. The Captain knew I would be killed for this ritual. He suggested it might be better to present me to the Queen of England. I would represent a symbol of goodwill between their two countries. Captain Forbes later called me "a gift from the King of the Blacks to the Queen of the Whites."

When the Captain left the palace, he led me by the hand. My body shook as we walked away because I feared King Ghezo would change his mind and take me back. Many other pale men followed us. I believed Captain Forbes must be very powerful, or a king in his own country, to have so many men march behind him. All I had was the white ceremonial dress I wore.

Even though I had never met anyone like him before, and frightened as I was, I felt safer with him than with King Ghezo of Dahomey.

We rode on a large wagon for days until we came to a big river. There I saw the largest boat I had ever seen. It was taller than five men and had great sheets of fabric hanging from long, wooden arms, like skinny trees. Captain Forbes held my hand as he guided me up a narrow board over the water.

When the boat began to move, I fell over, and the sailors laughed. Captain Forbes said something to me I did not understand, but it sounded comforting. He reached down a hand to help me up, but I stood up on my own, and he smiled. The big boat sailed to the city of Badagry.

The Point of No Return
Badagry

At the port city of Badagry, Captain Forbes brought me to the Church Missionary Society. Some of the women there spoke Yoruba, my language. They explained that Captain Forbes was from a country very far away called England. It was not part of our homeland in Africa. He was going to take me to meet their Queen.

The Missionary women gave me a new dress. It had so much more cloth than what we usually wear. Mrs. Vidal, the wife of the Missionary leader, made a painting of me in my new outfit.

We went to a building they called a church, and this Missionary leader poured some water over my head. He then announced that my name would be Sarah Forbes Bonetta. It upset me when he wet my hair, but the Captain smiled, and that reassured me.

My parents had named me Aina, but Captain Forbes wanted to label me Sarah. Everyone else might have called me by this strange name, but I still thought of myself as Aina.

Sometimes in the evenings I would sing my songs. Some of the others joined in and sang with me. This made me very happy.

The nice ladies at the Church Missionary Society began teaching me your English-tongue to prepare me for my voyage to England. They told me I learned very fast. While my English has improved greatly over the years since then, I have recorded my earliest crude attempts at speaking just as I remembered them. Looking back, I realized how ill-formed my sentences sounded at the time, but they were my best attempts.

To reward me for my good work the nice ladies would take me on walks about the city. One day we went

toward the edge of the great water
that surrounds all our lands. I saw a
column of clay just about as tall as me,
and I ran toward it. "Stop," they
shouted. "Do not touch that!"

"What this?" I asked. I looked inside
and saw dark water.

"That is poison, my child," one of the women told me. "The white men make us drink that before they put us on the ships."

It was the first time I heard the phrase "white men," and I asked what that meant. The ladies told me that the people with the pale skin are called "white," and those of us with regular skin are called "black." This made no sense to me as the white people looked pink, and we black people looked golden brown.

"Come with us," one of the ladies said as she grabbed my hand and led me to a wooden structure by the water's edge.

"What this?" I asked. It looked like a nice place to walk along the shore.

"The white men take our people to other countries to work for them. This is the last thing they see before being put on a boat and leaving Africa forever. It is called 'The Point of No Return.'"

Taking people away from their home seemed very cruel. It had happened to me when King Ghezo captured my family. "Why they do that?"

One woman stared down at me with tears in her eyes. "The white men think they are better than us. They think we are theirs to enslave and perform their hard, hard labours."

That sounded very, very wrong. How could white men believe they were superior? Why would they take people from their homes and send them far away? Those who traded with King Ghezo were not such good people.

"Never," the woman continued, "Never walk along here alone. Do you understand?"

I did not understand, but I nodded my head anyway. This walk along the water seemed pleasant, but she told

me bad things happened here. Perhaps it would be best not to return.

A Sea Voyage
Sailing on the HMS Bonetta

One day, Captain Forbes came to visit me at the Church Missionary Society. He spoke with the ladies who took care of me. One of them approached and told me, "Your Captain Forbes is ready to take you to meet his Queen. You will go back to the big boat that brought you here. He will take you across the great water. You learn much and come back here to teach us, yes?"

I hugged her and walked out with Captain Forbes. He led me back to the big boat. As we stood on the platform beside it, he pointed up and asked, "Can you read that, Sarah?"

I did not know what he asked. The ladies at the Church Missionary Society had taught me some of the English-tongue, but I did not yet understand all the words. After a few seconds, I shook my head.

"It says, *HMS Bonetta.* I named you for my ship." He smiled. "My men are not accustomed to having a young woman such as yourself onboard. We have fashioned you a room for yourself. Come,"–he held out his hand–"let me show you."

He had already chosen the name Sarah for me, but in my mind, I was still Aina. To that he added his own name, Forbes, like he had taken possession of me. Sandwiched in between he put Bonetta. I had wondered where the word came from. While it might have been pride that led him to label me after his ship, I would have preferred not to share my name with a non-living thing.

Together we walked up the wooden planks to his big boat. The other white men smiled at me, and some bowed very slightly to me.

"Why they bend like that?" I asked, using some of the words the nice ladies had taught me.

"It is a sign of respect," he said. "I told them you are a princess, and my people show their respect by bending, but we call it bowing."

Back in my home town, when people wanted to show respect, they bent very far, almost to the ground. Perhaps these men only bent just a little bit because I was just a little person.

My room was small and dark. It was not much better than the prison at King Ghezo's palace. But here I had freedom. I could walk outside at any time I wanted.

The day we sailed away, I stood with Captain Forbes as the coast of Africa disappeared behind us. This frightened me because I had never been in a place where I could not see land. I

squeezed the Captain's hand, and he
gently squeezed mine.

He had shown me concern and respect,
and I began to think better of the
white Captain Forbes. As the days
went on and nothing bad happened, I
no longer felt he would harm me.

At night in my room I would sing my
songs. It was all I had from my life in
Oke-Odan.

Captain Forbes told me that white
people referred to moon cycles as
'months.' The Yoruba system had 13
osu (months) instead of only 12 per
year (*odun*). Our counting began at
the beginning of time, almost 10,000
years ago, but the white people
counted from the birth of their Lord,
Jesus. We had sailed from Africa during the seventh month, called July, in
the year numbered 1850.

The other white men spoke with me and helped me to learn more of your English-tongue. By the time we reached England, I could speak with them quite well.

Everyone on the big boat got very excited when we finally approached their land of England. The Captain ordered large pieces of colourful cloth to be raised. He told me they were flags used to identify the ship and the country it came from.

As we got nearer the land, people stood on the cliffs cheering and waving at us. I waved back at them.

It felt good to see land again, even if it was not my own home in Africa. Unlike all the villages I had ever seen, the people in this England built their homes very close to each other.

I pointed to the crowded houses and asked the Captain, "What is this?"

"Gravesend," he replied.

From the words I had already learned, Gravesend did not sound like a happy place to me.

My First Home in England
Winkfield Place

Captain Forbes and I rode in one of their large wagons to a town called Winkfield Place. Along the way he pointed to a tall stone structure on a hill. He said that it was Windsor Palace, one of the Queen's homes.

It was much bigger than King Ghezo's palace in Abomey. The stones looked very cold from a distance.

"I meet the Queen?" I asked.

He smiled. "Soon. Very soon, my princess." He squeezed my hand. "First, I have to let the Queen know we want to see her, and then she has to invite us."

"That seems very wearisome," I responded.

"Yes, it is, Sarah, but the Queen has rules we must follow, whether we agree with them or not."

The white people had so many peculiar rules. The Church Missionary Society had rules. The *Bonetta* had rules. The Queen has rules. Rules, rules, rules.

Captain Forbes introduced me to his wife, whom he only called "Mrs. Forbes." She asked me to call her "mama." At first, I did not like to call her that because she was not my own mother. After a while, I could tell she regarded me like her own child, and I felt better about calling her mama. She had no children of her own, and I believed it made her feel better to think of me as her daughter.

Mrs. Forbes taught me more of your English-tongue, the ways of the writing letters and words, but most importantly, she introduced me to the music-making piano.

The fancy box had black and white pieces of wood called "keys" that made a sound when you pressed them. She showed me how to press the keys in different orders to make songs. After a while, I was able to play some of my songs for Mrs. Forbes.

She taught me a piece called "Twinkle, Twinkle, Little Star." I played that song whenever I had a chance.

Captain Forbes spent most of his time in a room he called "the library." He sat at a great table and used a feather dipped in black liquid to create the letters, just like Mrs. Forbes had taught me. He told me he was writing his story about the trip to Africa and the visit to King Ghezo so that other people could learn of his travels.

Mrs. Forbes taught me how to make the curtsey, the way women show respect in England. Instead of merely bending at the waist like the men, a woman places one foot behind the other and makes herself lower. She also nods her head forward. This seemed much more like the display of respect I remember from home.

The first time I tried the curtsey, I fell over. Mrs. Forbes did not laugh at me, but she did hide her mouth with a hand. I tried it again with more success. Once I had mastered the movement, she suggested I hold the sides of my dress out as far as I could while I lowered myself.

This seemed silly, and I asked her why we must do this. She turned her face up and looked far away. "That's just the way we've always done it, I suppose so," she explained.

Rules, rules, rules.

On the first day of the month they called November, Captain Forbes called me into his library. "Sarah," he began, "I have some very good news for you. The Queen's husband, Prince Albert, has invited us to meet him at Windsor Palace. That was the stone castle I showed you when we first came to Winkfield Place."

"I meet the Queen?"

"Most likely, but the Prince wants to meet you first," he told me.

This made me think, "If he is husband of the Queen, why not King?"

"Yes," Captain Forbes hesitated. "That is a very good question. You are such a smart girl." He put a finger to the side of his face. Perhaps it helped him to think. "Prince Albert is not the King because he did not inherit the throne from his father. He only married Victoria after she had already become Queen."

"To take throne?" I asked.

Captain Forbes made a little laugh. "No, Sarah. He married the Queen because he loved her, and she loved him."

That seemed such a silly idea. People should not get married just because they love each other. They should also get married to acquire property and have children.

Preparing To Meet the Queen
Windsor Castle

Mrs. Forbes took me to a building in Winkfield Place that sold clothing for girls. I had never seen so many dresses in one place before. And they were so colourful and frilly.

She let me choose a simple piece with blue and white stripes. Another item Mrs. Forbes picked out for me was an outer garment called a "coat." She told me that in England, there are times of year when the weather is cold, much colder than I was used to in Africa.

The way English women dressed seemed very silly to me. Around their middle, they bind themselves with a very tight piece of fabric called a "corset," but then they make their bottoms look bigger with a device called a "bustle."

Some of the women wore a stiff frame under their dress to make it appear even bigger at the bottom. None of this made sense to me. It made them look like one of their time-keeping devices, an hourglass.

In Africa, we appreciated the sunshine and dressed lightly. We honoured the mother earth by dressing in her colours, and our robes flowed with our bodies as we walked.

On the day they labelled 9 November 1850, Captain Forbes and I rode to Windsor Castle in his fancy cart. He wore his Navy Captain's uniform, and I had the clothes Mrs. Forbes had purchased for me.

When we arrived at the great stone building, soldiers in bright red uniforms greeted us and led the Captain and me to a cold, stone room with many pieces of cloth hanging from the walls and ceiling.

A tall man with bushy hair entered, followed by many soldiers. He walked up to us and said, "Captain Forbes."

The Captain bent slightly, much the way people had bent to him. He had told me it was respectful. "Your Highness," he said when he stood up.

"Is this the child?" The tall man pointed at me. The way he spoke the English-tongue sounded different, like he was angry or in a hurry.

"Yes, Your Highness," Captain Forbes placed his hand on my back. "May I present Sarah Forbes Bonetta."

I did not know what to do, and everyone in the cold room stared at me. Thinking I should show this tall, bushy man respect, I bent at my middle, making the little bow.

Loud laughter echoed. Perhaps I should have made the curtsey instead. I took up the sides of my dress with my hands, put one foot behind me, and bent my knees. When I stood up, I could see the tall man smiling. "You are quite proper, I see. Captain Forbes and his wife have taught you well."

I smiled up at him because I felt proud to be a good student.

He looked down at me with concern. "Captain Forbes, what is that scarring about her mouth?" He pointed to his own cheek.

"The Yoruba people mark their faces to indicate social position."

"And what do her marks indicate?"

"She is the daughter of the tribe's chief."

"Oh? A princess, then?" The tall man bowed and extended his hand to me. "I am pleased to meet you, Princess Sarah."

I wanted to correct him and say, "My name is Aina," but the feeling of someone calling me 'Princess' surpassed all other sentiments.

Captain Forbes pushed me forward. "Let the Prince take your hand, Sarah."

I allowed the tall man, whom Captain Forbes called the Prince to place my hand in his. He kissed my hand lightly before letting it go.

"Please to follow me, and I shall take you to meet my wife, the Queen."

My First Visit with the Queen

Windsor Castle

We followed the Prince through the hallways and arrived in a very fancy room. Shiny gold reflected from many of the surfaces, and the chairs had thick cushions. Paintings of people hung from the walls, and a large mirror hung over the fireplace.

"We shall wait here," the Prince instructed. A few minutes later, a door at the other end of the room opened. Through the door stepped a servant. Following her, a woman about my own height entered. Behind her, a boy and girl slightly older than me, and behind them, more servants.

"Albert, is this the African girl?" the woman asked. Even though she did not wear a crown or royal robes, I knew she must be the Queen.

"Yes, Your Majesty," he pushed me a bit forward, "this is Princess Sarah Forbes Bonetta."

"Princess?" the Queen squeaked. She turned to me. "Are you a real princess, young lady?"

I looked up to Captain Forbes because I did not know how to answer the Queen's question. He stepped forward and stood next to me.

"Your Majesty," he made a slight bend. "These marks"–he pointed to the scars on my cheeks–"indicate Sarah's rank in her tribe. She is, indeed, a princess in her own realm."

The Queen smiled at me. "Approach, my dear," she instructed.

Captain Forbes looked down at me and nodded. I took a few tentative steps toward the Queen. Before I got too close, I remembered to curtsey before her as a sign of respect.

"How cultured she is, Albert. Would you not say so?" the Queen smiled.

"Yes, my dear. I have found her quite well-educated," the Prince answered.

The Queen drew one of her cold, tiny fingers across my cheeks along the scars. "Fascinating," she whispered. "Please remove your bonnet for us."

I untied the ribbons from the little hat and held it in my hand. My hair sprung forth.

"Oh, my, Albert! What lovely hair she has," the Queen observed. "And her earrings are so... so... foreign." Her head turned one way and the other as she looked at me. "Yes, we believe she demonstrates the true Negro type."

I had never heard that word before, and I turned to Captain Forbes. "*Negro?*" I asked.

The room fell silent. Several people coughed into their fists. I hoped I had not done something bad.

"Sometimes people use that word to indicate black people, the ones from Africa, such as yourself," he explained.

"Yes, my dear," the Queen added, "We are merely referring to your delightful ancestry. We do not see many children like yourself here in England." She turned to the Prince. "Albert, we believe we would like to have a photographic portrait with Princess Sarah. Could you please see to that?"

The Prince bent again and left the room.

"Where is your family, my dear?" the Queen asked. Again, I looked to Captain Forbes.

"Your Majesty, Sarah's family was captured by King Ghezo of Dahomey a few years ago. Sarah is the only one to survive. I requested her to be a gift to you as a sign of goodwill between the King and yourself."

"A gift? Captain Forbes, we cannot receive another human being as a gift," the Queen seemed upset. "We put an end to slavery in our realm years ago, and we cannot–in all good conscience–accept her as a *gift*. However,"–she smiled–"we can accept her as our *guest*." She looked at me directly. "Would you like to stay with us here at Windsor for a few days?"

Again, I looked up at the Captain. He smiled and nodded. "Yes, Your Majesty," I responded.

The Prince returned. "All is prepared," he stated.

"Cut Off Head!"

Mayall Photography Studio

Accompanied by the Prince, Captain Forbes and I followed the band of servants out of the stone castle gate. The town of Windsor was much less crowded than Gravesend, and it had a nicer sounding name as well.

We stopped at one of the shops along the road. I pointed up at the sign and asked the Captain, "What that say?"

"It reads, 'John J.E. Mayall, Daguerreotype Institution,'" he responded.

"'Gerra type?" I shot back.

He smiled and answered, "It's a new type of portrait. The man will use a box to capture your image, and it will appear on a glass plate."

This sounded dangerous. I had been the prisoner of King Ghezo for a long time. "No wish capture again, Captain Forbes," I informed him.

"No, no," he laughed. "He does not take one prisoner. There is a mechanism within the box that creates an image."

"Like magic painting?" I asked.

He smiled and said, "Yes. Like magic painting."

We entered the shop and a handsome white man in a dark suit stepped forward quickly.

"Your majesty," he said before he made a bow to the Prince. "Welcome to my Windsor studio. What is the purpose of this unexpected visit?"

"Good morning, Mr. Mayall," the Prince responded. "My wife the Queen has requested a portrait of our little visitor here." He pointed a hand toward me.

"Ahhhhh!" sang Mr. Mayall. "I have never seen a specimen so lovely before. Does she speak?"

"Yes, I speak," I announced, somewhat annoyed at the idea he thought I might be stupid.

"And she understands English!" the photographer exclaimed. "How delightful!"

The Prince explained, "Mr. Mayall, our friend Sarah is a princess in her home country. Please treat her accordingly."

"Yes, of course." He bent a bit. "This way, Your Highness." He turned to the Prince. "Your Highnesses."

He pulled aside a dark curtain and we stepped into a large apartment with many pieces of furniture. On the wall I could see pictures of people, but they looked real. Only there was no colours, fainter than their already pale skin. I prayed that the magic box would not take my colour away.

I saw one picture of a man holding a large sword, like the ones used by King Ghezo's soldiers. In fear of my life I ran out, screaming "Cut off head! Cut off head!"

Captain Forbes followed quickly behind me. "Sarah, what is wrong?"

"Man with sword. Cut off head," I answered, shaking and trembling.

"No one is going to harm you, Sarah," the Captain said as he put his arms about me. "Look around. That man is not here. None of us has a sword. I promise you that as long as I am by your side, no one will ever hurt you again."

"The Clouds Fall"
Windsor Castle

I continued to live with the Forbes family, and Mrs. Forbes gave me daily lessons. Years later, someone told me that Queen Victoria herself paid for my boarding expenses.

The climate of England during the winter months was very different from that of Oke-Odan or King Ghezo's palace. At home, it was always warm and balmy, and we enjoyed feeling the sunshine on our skin. England was a very cold place, and I had to wear many layers to stay warm, especially when we went outdoors.

One morning, Captain Forbes told me, "Sarah, I have a big surprise for you. Today, we are going to visit with the Queen!"

That made me very happy. The Queen was closer to my height than the other people, and I enjoyed her company. We rode in Captain Forbes's carriage back to Windsor Castle, and the servants led us to the Queen's drawing room. The castle was even colder than the Forbes home. I shivered.

The Queen entered, and all the people bent toward her, and I made the same bend. She walked directly to me and took my hand.

"Good morning, princess," she said with a small smile. "How nice to see you again, Sally."

I turned to Captain Forbes. "Why does she say Sally? Aina… Sarah is my name."

The Queen began to laugh. "My child, we give all the people we care about a special, secret name." She held out a hand to me and I took it. "Let us go for a walk in the garden."

She led me through the castle and the servants opened the doors for us. We stepped outside and I pulled my coat around me even tighter.

When we walked, the grass made crunching noises under our feet. None of the trees had leaves. I felt badly that their crops had died.

We stepped up to an oval-shaped ring with a solid white surface. "What this?" I asked, pointing to the colourless area.

The Queen looked down and laughed, "We imagine you have never seen ice before." I shook my head. She pointed down. "This is water, but it is frozen."

"Frozen?" I had not yet learned that word.

"When water gets very, very cold, it turns solid. We say it is frozen," she explained.

I was very, very cold, and I hoped that I would not be frozen as well.

"Watch this," the Queen instructed. She dropped my hand and stepped onto the ice.

"Queen!" I screamed. "You fall into water!" I tried to reach out to her, but she slid away from me. This person must be very powerful to slide over the water without falling in.

She laughed at my words. "It is completely safe. The ice is solid. Come, join us." The Queen slid back to me and grabbed my hand. I wanted to run because I thought she might try to make me fall into the pond.

Before I had a chance to move, she pulled me toward her, and I stood with her on the ice. We did not fall into the water. Perhaps I was very powerful as well!

"Follow us," the Queen ordered. She began sliding about on the ice. I watched her move her feet from side to side.

When I started to move, I felt very shaky. One of my legs slipped out from under me and I fell to the ice. It was very, very cold and quite hard.

The Queen put a hand to her mouth to hide a smile. She slid up to me and extended her hand. I took it and she pulled me up. While we held hands, she guided me around the oval, and we both slid together.

Once I got used to it, the sliding became very fun! We chased each other about on the ice.

Something unseen touched me on the face. I could not see it, but I could feel it. When I turned to look, I felt it again. As it seemed to be coming from above, I looked up.

"The clouds fall!" I announced. It appeared the stuff from the sky fell upon us.

Again, the Queen laughed at my words. "We presume you have never experienced snow before." She held out her hand and several white flakes landed there. "This is also water."

"But it falls!"

"Yes, it falls, but it is frozen like this pond. Snow starts out in the sky, like rain." She lifted her hand to her mouth and licked the snow.

"No snow in Africa," I proclaimed.

"No, indeed." She lifted her face to the sky and stuck out her tongue.

I tried to imitate her, and a few pieces of the snow landed on my face and lips. It tasted just like cold water. I smiled.

Winter in England
Windsor Castle

Captain Forbes allowed me to remain with the Queen when he left for his home. It was then I first met the royal children.

Princess Alice seemed the closest in age to me. As I had no idea when I was born, Captain Forbes estimated 1843 as my birth year.

Prince Albert, whom they called "Bertie," and Princess Victoria, whom they called "Vicky," were slightly older, but the four of us played together in a large apartment they shared in the palace. A very nice woman named Mrs. Hull watched over us.

During one of the first afternoons at the castle, the Queen invited me to her sitting room. I recognized the object against the wall with a large mirror as a piano and stepped over to it.

As I admired the fancy instrument, she asked, "Do you know how to play?"

"Yes, Mrs. Queen. Mrs. Forbes teach me how. You want I show?"

The Queen smiled. "Yes, please. We are eager to hear your musical talents."

Instead of sitting on the bench, I stood at the right end of the keyboard and plunked out "Twinkle, Twinkle, Little Star."

"That's very good!" the Queen said as she clapped her hands politely. "Please let us join you." She sat on the bench and played keys to the left of me as I performed the song again. The Queen made many more sounds than I did, and she used both her hands at the same time. As I watched her, I wished that I would be able to do that some-day. She turned to me and asked, "Do you know other pieces?"

I nodded my head and began playing some of the songs from home. When I finished, the Queen stood very quietly and put a hand on my shoulder.

"Those are very intriguing melodies, indeed. Could you show us how to play them?"

We spent the rest of the day playing the piano together.

When I returned to the children's room, I found Vicky and Alice holding some strange objects. They looked like shrunken miniature people but made from sticks and little bones.

"Child of wood?" I asked. Back in Africa, we had similar toys we wrapped in cloth and pretended they were our babies.

"We call them dolls," Vicky responded. "This is my little one. Would you like a dolly of your own?"

How exciting! It had been years since I had my own baby toy. If I had a new one, I would never be lonely again. The Princess walked to a cabinet and removed another one of the small figures and handed it to me. It had a plain dress, and her hair stuck to the side of her head. Unfortunately, the skin looked very England pale, not like my African skin at all.

"Thank you, Princess Vicky," I said with a bit of a frown.

"Oh, how silly of me!" She exclaimed. The Princess took the doll back and walked to a table on the other side of the room.

I watched as she took a thin stick and applied some kind of colouring to the doll. When she handed the figure back to me, her skin shone golden brown, closer to my own but still the shape of the face still resembled the other girls.

"Oh, thank you, Princess!" I said, wishing to be polite. I believed she truly meant her gift to be considerate. It did not resemble my "child of wood" from back home, but now I had a constant companion.

"When she handed the figure back to me, her skin shone golden brown, similar to mine."

"You are very welcome. Do you wish to give her a name?" the other girl asked.

It did not take very long for me to think. "Aina," I announced. "This is Princess Aina."

One of the things in the palace I found intriguing were the small black rocks called "coal" that held fire inside of them. When the rooms got cold, which was most of the time, servants would bring big metal buckets full of the black rocks to us. They would put them in the hole in the wall called the "fireplace." This mystified me because at home we only used fire for cooking or light at night.

One morning, the Queen's husband, Prince Albert, appeared in our apartment. "Come, children, we are going for a ride," he announced.

The other three began cheering and smiling.

"Can Princess Sarah come with us, Father?" asked Princess Victoria. "We would enjoy it so much more immensely if she could accompany us."

"Of course, Vicky," her father responded. "It was my intention to include her. Come."

We marched in a line like soldiers and followed him out of a palace gate, where I saw a small horse tethered to a small cart. It was not as grand as those I had ridden in with Captain Forbes, and it had no cover.

The Tall Prince helped us each in turn into the small cart. He then led the small horse along the paths. We cheered and laughed. The others began waving their hands as if a large crowd of people stood watching us. I pretended we were passing by the pitiful palace of the old King Ghezo, and I waved and cheered as well. It was the most fun I had ever had.

Later that evening, my head felt funny. My eyes would not stop tearing, and fluid ran from my nose. One of the servants used a cloth to remove the excess moisture on my face.

In the morning, I began coughing and sneezing rather violently, and my belly hurt. When the servants appeared, one of them suggested calling for the Prince.

The Tall Prince approached me and stared at my head from a few different angles. "Call for Mr. Clark, the Physician," he said.

A few minutes later, a skinny man with a head like an egg entered the room. "What seems to be the matter, Your Highness?" he asked the Prince.

"Our visitor from Africa seems unwell this morning. Could you please examine her?" the Prince asked.

Mr. Clark approached me slowly, as if I were going to bite him or scratch him like a large cat. He studied my head, much the way the Prince did. When he put his hand near me, I pulled back because I did not want to be touched by this strange man.

"Young lady," Mr. Clark said, "I cannot adequately provide a diagnosis without being able to make contact with you."

"Sarah, please allow Mr. Clark to touch you. He is only here to help," Prince Albert said.

I nodded my head and the physician approached me again. This time, he pulled his hand away from me at the last moment, as if the strange man did not want to touch the strange girl.

Mr. Clark turned to the Prince. "I believe the harsh English climate is unsuitable for African people. Perhaps it might be best to return the girl to her natural habitat."

I had no idea what "natural habitat" meant, but I felt too ill to ask any questions.

"Sarah, we shall take you back to stay with Captain Forbes while the Queen and I decide how best to settle this matter," the Prince informed me.

When I returned to the Captain's home, Mrs. Forbes told me he had sailed back to Africa to continue the work he had begun. I looked forward to returning to my former home and to seeing Captain Forbes.

A Visit with Prince Albert
Windsor Castle

The good Mrs. Forbes kept the house very warm with a big fire in the fireplace. That helped me sleep through the night without coughing or sneezing.

In the morning, Mrs. Forbes woke me from a dream about my home village of Oke-Odan. The images of my family lingered in my head.

"You were singing in your sleep, my dearest Sarah," she told me.

I must have been dreaming of my young days as Aina and the old songs as well. "Sorry, Mrs. Forbes," I said.

"Oh, no, dear child!" she replied. "It was most lovely. I hated to awaken you, but a carriage from Windsor Palace is here to take you."

I dressed as quickly as I could, hugged Mrs. Forbes, and stepped outside where the royal carriage awaited. A uniformed servant had to lift me into the box. I truly felt like a princess, but a princess with an illness.

Upon our arrival at Windsor Castle, the servant led me to a room with many books. A few minutes later, the Tall Prince entered.

"Good morning, Princess Sarah," he greeted me with a small bend. "And how are we this fine day?"

My head felt heavy and water beaded up under my nose. "Not well, Mr. Prince. I have sickness."

"Homesickness?" he asked. I had not heard that word before, but illness caused by one's own home sounded quite dreadful. "Mr. Clark has recommended we provide a more appropriate atmosphere for you. Tomorrow, you will ride to London, where a ship is waiting to take you to Africa."

I stood and made the curtsey. "Thank you, Mr. Prince. Captain Forbes boat?"

The Prince stopped smiling. His face seemed dark. "Sarah, I have some rather distressing news for you. Word has arrived that your dear Captain Forbes has died in Africa."

A few tears fell from my eyes. I would never see the man who had rescued me from King Ghezo again. I had already lost my parents and all my family. My insides felt tight and dark.

"But I have something for you. A special gift," the Prince told me. He stepped to a table with books on it and took one from the top of a stack. The Prince knelt slightly and presented a very heavy volume to me.

"What this?" I asked. At that point, I had not yet mastered reading of the English-tongue and could not understand the printing on the cover.

"Why, this is the journal that Captain Forbes kept of his journeys to Dahomey, where he first found you."

I took the big book from him. "Thank you, Mr. Prince." What good was a book for a young woman who could not yet read?

"Look inside," he said, and I opened the front cover. There was a drawing of King Ghezo, and I shut the book with a bang. "Let me show you." The Prince opened it to the middle, and there was a drawing of me. "It reads, 'Sarah Forbes Bonetta, The African Captive.'"

I started to smile when I saw myself as Aina, but then I had to wonder, "What mean 'captive'?"

"Ah, yes," the Prince stroked his chin with one hand. Perhaps it helped him to think harder. "A captive is a person who has been taken against their will. A prisoner, so to speak."

"I no captive!" I blurted out.

"No, not now, your Highness," the Prince responded, "but when Captain

Forbes first found you, you were a captive."

"King Ghezo!"

"Yes, King Ghezo held you prisoner, and Captain Forbes made him release you. Now you are here, no longer a captive."

I smiled again. "No captive!" I looked again at the large book. This must have been what Captain Forbes had written all those evenings he had spent at his desk. It made me think that perhaps someday I would learn writing and make a book about my life.

"But our cold, damp English climate is no place for a young princess like yourself," the Prince advised me. "We have arranged passage for you to return to your native African continent."

"I go back to King Ghezo?" The thought frightened me. I never wanted to see that horrible man again.

"No, no. Of course not," he comforted me. "We have decided to send you to a country called Sierra Leone. You will meet people who look more like you, but they will speak more like us."

"The English-tongue?" I asked.

He nodded. "The English-tongue, indeed."

The Crystal Palace
London

When it came time for me to depart, Mrs. Forbes gave me very long hugs. I know she had been deeply affected by the death of her husband. We spoke of him at length the previous evening. Even though I was not their daughter, I believed Mrs. Forbes had always thought of me as her own.

"Stay healthy, Sarah. Remember us, please, as we will never forget you. You are always welcome to stay with me should you return to England."

Many tears made our faces very wet. I would never forget her husband, Captain Forbes, the man who rescued me from King Ghezo.

A carriage took me from Windsor through the early-morning fog to the metropolis of London, where I was to embark for Sierra Leone. When we stopped, a surprise awaited me.

Dressed in his shiny military uniform, the Tall Prince greeted me with a bow and a grand smile.

"Welcome to London, Princess Sarah." He reached out his hand and I took it as I departed the carriage. "I have something I wish to show you."

The Tall Prince had always treated me like one of his own children, even though he had so many of his own. His smile did not fade as we walked to another carriage.

London was much bigger than Windsor. So many people! The buildings were even closer together. I did not like it very much.

We stopped near a big open area. I could see a very large building with no walls! The sides had only glass. How amazing!

"Welcome to the Crystal Palace, Princess Sarah," the Tall Prince said.

These English people had more palaces than old King Ghezo back in Dahomey. I didn't think I could live in such a place with no walls. Everyone would look in as they walked past.

The Tall Prince led me to the entrance. As we passed, people would bend to him and me.

"My wife, the Queen, thought I needed a project to keep me busy." He indicated the palace with the sweep of an arm. "And this is what I have done.

We call it 'The Great Exhibition.'
Come."

The two of us walked up to the glass
walls and I could see my reflection. I
looked taller than I had remembered.

Inside the Crystal Palace there were
trees and birds and many, many people. Some were dressed in very fancy
clothes I had never seen before.
Wrapped in long, colourful fabrics,
some wore tall, funny hats.

For hours we walked about, looking at displays from far-off lands, including my Africa. We stopped at the display from Sierra Leone, my new home-to-be, and I met some very nice people. I hoped the people there would be just as nice.

Most of the time in England, I stood out because of my darker skin. However, the crowd inside the Crystal Palace included many different skin colours, and no one looked at me any differently.

I saw all kinds of animals, big and small, from just about everywhere. There were enormous, grey elephants from India, large, ferocious lions from Southern Africa, scaly, long-toothed alligators from Florida, and funny-looking, colourful lizards from Asia.

The Tall Prince seemed to marvel at all the fascinating new mechanical devices. One curious apparatus allowed people to transmit images scratched into thin, metal sheets across the room by some invisible power called electricity. We also looked at "The Trophy Telescope" and the Tall Prince explained one could peer through its glass and see the stars up close. I told him I could see the stars at night just fine, and I did not need a giant machine to look for me.

However, one particular thing enthralled me like nothing else I saw that day: a large chunk of glass that shined like a thousand brilliant rainbows.

"That is the Koh-I-Noor Diamond," the Tall Prince informed me. "It is from Persia, and its name means 'Mountain of Light.' When we took the Punjab region recently, the stone came to us."

I continued to stare at the piece of glass that gave me such delight. Eventually, the Tall Prince pulled me away and we looked at even more displays.

When I got hungry, we stopped for Bath buns and tea.

Some time in the late afternoon I began to get tired, and I started to slow down. The Tall Prince said, "Perhaps we should get you to your ship before you fall asleep or it sets sail without you!"

Returning to Africa
Freetown, Sierra Leone

The Tall Prince took me to meet Reverend Schmid, the man whom Queen Victoria had chosen to accompany me to Sierra Leone. He was shorter and thinner than the Prince.

We boarded another carriage, one bound for the sadly-named Gravesend. He barely acknowledged my being there. Most of the time he chattered with his very quiet wife about the dreaded dangers of Africa, as it was to be his first voyage. The poor woman could only nod while the Reverend went on about such things as "the fever" and how other missionaries had referred to Sierra Leone as "the white man's grave."

My memories of Oke-Odan were of beauty and peace, but King Ghezo had killed my family and held me captive for years. However, he treated Captain Forbes rather well. I do not know where this particular man heard bad things about my home, but at least he did not have to worry about being captured, sold, or presented as a gift to the Queen.

At the port, we boarded the *Bathurst*, a ship slightly smaller than Captain Forbes's *Bonetta*. The little room I had to sleep in seemed more like a shelf in a closet than a proper chamber. I had to spend most of the month's voyage in that small enclosure as the sea roiled and the winds blew without mercy.

The port of Freetown seemed much smaller than the English cities, but it felt more comfortable to me, especially since I had once again returned to my native African soil. The Reverend and his wife escorted me to the Church Missionary Society, where we met Reverend Henry Venn. Unlike the small and timid Reverend Schmid, Venn spoke loudly and forcefully.

I did not know it at the time, but I later found out that Reverend Venn had advocated for having more local African people run the colony and that it should produce cotton as a crop that could be sold to raise money. He also wanted to educate all its citizens, including girls and women.

At the Female Institution in Freetown, I studied with other African girls whose families wanted them educated in the manner English people had declared "proper." What I did not realize then was that the school charged money for this education and boarding. Unknown to me at the time, Queen Victoria herself had paid for my tuition and room. In fact, a portrait of the Queen hung over my bed in the room where I slept.

Some of the English missionaries looked at us native girls off the end of their pink, little noses and often referred to us as "primitive" or "savages." When those of us who spoke African tongues talked amongst ourselves, the teachers would inevitably reprimand us, scolding, "We speak only English here!"

The light-skinned English people staff taught us their way to speak, their way to dress, and their way to worship. They made us wear English dresses, English bonnets (much like what I had worn at Windsor), and sing English hymns. In the evenings, I would sing my old songs from Oke-Odan just to remind myself.

As I had already spent time with English people, I learned their English-tongue faster than my school-mates. While the other students enjoyed listening to my stories of meeting Queen Victoria and Prince Albert, the teachers would turn their heads away and make funny little noises, as if it made them upset to hear such things. The school had a piano, and they allowed me to play upon it from time to time, demon-strating the music the Queen had taught me.

We studied from *Murray's English Grammar*, and I finally learned how to read the symbols on paper just like the English people. Queen Victoria sent me letters every month or so, and I discovered how to make the symbols so that I could reply to her about my life in Freetown.

The English lady who ran the school, Miss Julia Sass, seemed quite proud of my progress. She would invite me to her home whenever she had visitors as a demonstration of how well her students performed. Miss Sass smiled and used fancy words when she told

them of my visits with the Queen and Prince Albert.

On the Queen's birthday, I hosted a "tea party" for 33 of the girls at the school. We drank African tea and sang *God Save the Queen*, first in the English-tongue, then we each took turns singing in our native tongues: Kru, Mendi, Egba, Egbado, and Yoruba. Miss Sass and the other white ladies did not seem happy about that.

News came to us that King Ghezo had attacked another Yoruba village, Abe-okuta, which was not far from my beloved home, Oke-Odan. Some of the people from the Church Missionary Society had been there attempting to establish a mission, and Samuel Crowther, the father of one of the girls I knew, Abigail, had been killed defending the village. I comforted Abigail knowing how it felt to have one's father killed by King Ghezo.

I looked on the map of Africa in our classroom to determine how far away Dahomey was from Freetown. No matter how I measured it, there was no distance that felt safe enough. As long as King Ghezo lived, I would not sleep comfortably.

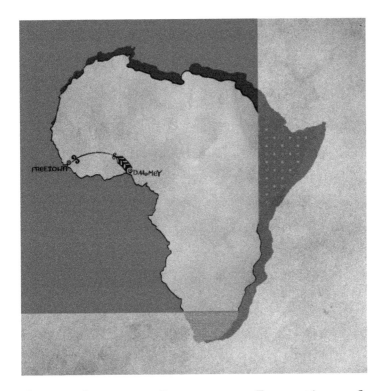

Over the next few years I continued my studies and learned as much as I could. Reverend Venn wanted us to become teachers ourselves, so that we could help educate our African brothers and sisters.

At one of Miss Sass's events, she presented an honoured guest, African missionary and businessman James Pinson Labulo Davies. He had been promoting trade along the African coast and stopped at Freetown along his voyage. Once again, I had been invited to represent the students.

Mr. Davies told us he had attended a Freetown school in his youth. After graduating, he joined the Royal Navy and worked his way up to Lieutenant, a rank of junior command. He asked many questions concerning the school, the other students, the teachers, and clerical staff. I answered as best I could, hoping to be a good representative of the Female Institution. To me, he was just another guest in a long line of visitors, but little did I know that it was not the last time we would meet.

A Letter from the Queen
Freetown, Sierra Leone

Over the next few years, I continued my studies at the Female Institution in Freetown. My ability to speak the English-tongue progressed greatly, and after a while I had mastered the nuances of your flat and wooden communication.

Miss Sass taught me the French-tongue, and she also provided music lessons. However, she became ill and had to travel to Europe for her health. Perhaps she suffered from a similar condition to mine in which foreign climates did not agree with her. In her absence, the wife of Reverend Dicker continued my schooling.

Many young women students came to the school, but they stayed only for a few months or a year at most. This situation presented difficulties for me to make lasting friendships.

One day, in my twelfth year, Miss Sass returned to Freetown, and I felt blessed to have my favourite instructor return. Soon after, she received a letter from a Mrs. Harriet Lepel Phipps, one of the Queen's confidential attendants. In her letter, Mrs. Phipps notified us that I was to be returned to England at once by Her Majesty's command.

We had no idea why the Queen would summon me with such urgency. In the month of June, I set off with Reverend Dicker and his wife. Students and teachers from the Female Institution came to the docks to see us off. Miss Sass fussed over my luggage, checking and re-checking that all the presents for Queen Victoria had been packed. Because I could now read the English letters, I saw the name *Hope* on the side of the ship. Hope is a good thing, and I prayed that it would carry me safely back to England.

Unlike previous ships on which I had travelled, this one had no sails to catch the wind. Reverend Dicker explained that heated water made some special wheels–called gears– turn, which moved the ship through the water. Without wind and sails or oarsmen, it seemed mystical and scientific.

The room I stayed in was larger than the one on the *Bathurst*. Beside a small bed, there was a small table, and a small chair. I had brought the picture of Queen Victoria with me, and it sat on the table. Reverend Dicker would read the Bible with me every day.

Meals were small and tasteless. My dress seemed much looser by the time we reached Gravesend. The Dickers accompanied me to the dock. We boarded a carriage bound for London.

The sea journey had exhausted me, and I slept during the ride. We stopped at a brick building in Salisbury Square. A sign read "Church Missionary Society."

Reverend Dicker and his wife escorted me inside. Standing by a desk stood a white man with a white beard and white hair.

"*Pehleh oh!*" he said with a deep, gruff voice.

I smiled because he spoke my native Yoruba-tongue.

"*Kaabo, oluwa,*" I responded, happy to hear someone I could easily understand. None of the other white people spoke our black tongues.

"I know your name is Sarah, but the Queen refers to you as Sally," he said. "How would you prefer me to call you?"

"My name is Aina, but Captain Forbes changed it to Sarah. Sarah is fine, mister," I responded.

He laughed a jolly laugh. "Mister! She called me 'Mister'! Please call me James, young lady, Sarah."

"Yes, Mister James."

Once again he laughed. "Have you ever ridden in a train before, young Sarah?"

I had not yet seen a train, but I knew them to be large metal carriages that floated over the land and carried people long distances. I shook my head to indicate that I had not ridden in a train before.

"Then you are in for a most marvellous treat. We will travel to my little village of Gillingham, where you will stay with me and my family at our Palm Cottage."

Reverend Dicker and his wife bid me farewell, and I walked with my new caretaker. The carriage had left us on the north side of the big river that divided London. To get to the train, we needed to cross over the rushing waters to the south part of the city. I had never walked across a bridge before, and I stepped very carefully. Below us I could see the big river, and I did not want to fall in.

When we finally arrived at the end of the bridge, I could feel my heart beating quite rapidly. We continued on, and we climbed a long ramp to a building with the word "Waterloo Station" on it.

A large, black machine sat there with clouds forming at its nose. At first, it scared me because of the loud noises it made. I saw large wheels and small wheels. In the bin behind the big machine I saw a pile of the black rocks that have fire inside. At least the carriage would be warm!

We walked along its side, past many windows and doors. James helped me up some metal stairs and into a small room where we sat on cushioned benches.

Once we were seated, the carriage moved suddenly, and it scared me. Grabbing the cushion on which I sat provided some comfort and safety. I could see out the window the buildings moving away. We floated over the land very fast.

I thought of the ship that brought me back to England. "Excuse me, Mister James, does the train move because heated water makes those special wheels–gears–turn?"

"Why, yes it does! You are a very smart young lady, Young Sarah. By the way, I am more commonly known as Reverend Schoen, but I would like you to continue to call me James."

"Yes, Mister James," I said. He smiled.

Eventually I became accustomed to riding in the train. It was much smoother than any of the ships I had sailed upon. Instead of leaping up and plunging down unexpectedly with the ocean waves, the train rocked from side-to-side. As we passed through the English countryside, I saw various farms and quaint small towns.

Life at Palm Cottage
Gillingham

About an hour after we left London, the train stopped at the town of Gillingham. I found stepping down to the ground even more frightening than stepping up to the train. If it started moving too soon, I might fall. With assistance and reassurance from Reverend Schoen, I slowly returned to the ground.

A hired wagon transported us to the Schoen home. The family consisted of seven children, and their eldest son, Frederick, was closest to my age.

Even though so many people lived in the cottage, it was smaller than any of the other homes I have lived in England. There was only one bedroom for the boys and one for the girls, but I had a chamber all to myself in the rear overlooking a small garden.

Mrs. Schoen treated me like one of the family, assigning me chores and lessons. As I had learned the craft of sewing while in Sierra Leone, she had me repair all the garments that wanted attention. I did not mind because I could work by myself and did not need to interact with the others.

At first, I felt much like an outsider. Not just because of the colour of our skins, but because the nine of them had lived together for many years and I had only recently arrived.

After a while, the girls began to request my presence when they played their games, looked at books, or took long walks about the area. The boys did not approach me or even look at me. Perhaps I scared them as much as they scared me.

When I felt confident enough to bring up topics on my own, I asked Mrs. Schoen why the Queen requested my presence in England but not with her at the palace. Mrs. Schoen looked away and her mouth got tight. "You will have to ask Her Majesty yourself the next time you see her, young lady," she responded. Sometimes I forgot that visiting with the Queen was not so common for everyone else.

The Reverend Schoen had learned to speak several African languages. Because he could speak Yoruba with me, it helped improve my grasp on your English-tongue much more so.

Much of my free time I spent with my correspondence. The people I wrote to the most were Mrs. Forbes, Mrs. Phipps, the Queen's attendant, and Queen Victoria herself.

One day I received an invitation from Her Majesty to join her at the London residence, St. James Palace. I asked the Reverend Schoen to accompany me as I did not feel comfortable riding the train by myself.

Mrs. Phipps met us at the station, and we rode in her chariot. Windsor Palace, the location I had known the best, sat in the midst of a wooded area, but the London Palace was surrounded by city buildings. We travelled through the dirty streets and I saw many poor people and other children wearing tattered clothing along the way. At that point, I did not realize how fortunate I had been.

The Queen smiled upon seeing me. "Sally," she shouted, "how you have grown. And how slender you are!"

"Thank you, Mrs. Queen, Your Majesty," I responded and then performed the curtsey. "You are looking very well yourself." I knew from my training by the English ladies in Sierra Leone to return a compliment when one is given. "May I ask a question of you, Mrs. Queen?"

Her face tightened into a smile of amusement. "Yes, of course, my child. What is it you wish?"

"Why did you request me to return to England from Sierra Leone?"

"My dear Sally," she spoke in low tones, "your correspondence seemed to indicate your unhappiness with your situation in Africa. Out of concern, we ordered your return to England."

I performed the curtsey again. "Thank you so very much, Your Highness, but why did you send me to live with the Schoens at Palm Cottage so far away from you?"

The Queen giggled at my question. "You ask so many questions for such a young girl. It is believed that Reverend Schoen would be the best man to conduct your further education, and education is quite important, you know."

"Oh, thank you, Mrs. Queen." Again, I performed the curtsey. "He is very learned in my Yoruba-tongue and that makes it easier for us to speak together."

She asked me questions about my time in Sierra Leone and I told her as much as I could remember. When she inquired into my home life with the Schoens, I informed her the family had done everything it could to make me feel welcome.

As time went on, I learned to ride the train to London and back by myself. Reverend Schoen would give me books to read for the journey.

The Queen invited me to drink tea with her daughters in a room whose walls had many fabric paintings–called tapestries–and a large fireplace.

She proclaimed with delight, "How I am surrounded by princesses, one and all!"

Every so often, the Queen would send me dresses to wear, and I could see that the Schoen daughters looked upon these gifts with longing. I did not realize at that time that most people did not receive personal gifts from their monarch.

In return for all of the Queen's gifts to me, I sewed a pair of very colourful slippers for the Tall Prince. When the Queen saw them, she requested a pair for herself as well!

At one visit, the Queen allowed me to join her in the drawing room where her throne sat on a raised platform. The walls and curtains were a deep red, and almost everything else looked like gold.

She held audience with foreign dignitaries, members of her own government, and several ordinary citizens. The Queen treated each person with the same dignity and respect. Never would I forget how someone with such great powers could remain so humble in the presence of commoners.

I sat off to the side and observed the proceedings very quietly, feeling quite honoured to be a silent witness. Most of the people spoke in a manner I could not understand anyway.

Following these visits with Queen Victoria, I would return to Gillingham and the Schoens. While I much preferred the slower pace of life in the small town, I would fall asleep dreaming of attending the Queen in her London palace.

A Royal Wedding
London

During the next few years, I continued my studies, but every month or so I took the train to London. Sometimes we returned to Windsor Palace, but most of my visits with Her Majesty's family occurred in St. James Palace.

When the weather agreed with us, we would walk through the great park near the palace. Not far from St. James I discovered yet another palace called Buckingham. The grounds included woodlands and lakes. Sometimes we tried to catch the small animals we found. In the spring, we gathered flowers to present to the Queen.

One day during my fifteenth year, a parcel arrived at Palm Cottage from Her Majesty. Inside we found a portrait of a man named Prince Frederick William. His family ruled a land called Prussia. The Queen's oldest daughter,

Princess Victoria, would marry this man, and the Royal Family requested my presence at the ceremony.

Mrs. Phipps sent me a lovely pale, yellow dress to wear for the occasion. Princess Victoria wore a white gown trimmed with a great deal of lace, and she carried a bouquet of orange flowers. Behind her flowed a long trail of the same white fabric, and I helped hold it as she walked.

The Prince wore his military uniform, a dark blue tunic with gold trim and a silver sash. He looked so handsome!

Three of the Queen's sons—Princes Bertie, Arthur, and Leopold—wore strange outfits with what looked like a girl's skirt. When I mentioned this to Princess Alice, she told me it was traditional Highland dress from a region called Scotland. All the girls wore wreaths of flowers in our hair.

Hundreds of people from many countries attended the wedding. When I looked about the crowd, it appeared I was the only person from Africa. At first it did not occur to me, but as I met more and more people, I began to realize how much I stood out.

During my time in England, I had gotten accustomed to being different, as almost all the people I knew were white. But in this large assemblage, my difference appeared much greater. No one treated me any differently, but some people did stare. I could only presume they had never met someone of my culture before.

Princess Alice approached and gushed, "Isn't this so exciting?"

"Yes," I responded. "I am so happy to be part of your family's special event."

"You know," Alice continued, fanning herself with an intricately-carved ivory fan, "someday soon I will be having my own wedding. Several princes on the Continent have already sent me letters of inquiry upon the very subject!"

I felt happy for Princess Alice because she had the opportunity to marry a Prince. When I considered my own options, I believed there would be no queue of continental princes pressing their suit with me.

"How very happy I am for you, Alice. Truly I am," I told her.

"Oh, Sarah," she said, sounding a little sad. "I am sorry to be boasting in front of you, as I know you will most likely not have similar opportunities." She smiled. "But sometime soon you will want to marry as well. We will help find you a suitable husband."

I felt comforted by her words. While not one of Queen Victoria's own daughters, the royal princesses, the family had always treated me like one of their own.

However, I began to think how my life might have been if King Ghezo had not killed my family and held me prisoner in his Dahomey palace. Would I now be preparing to join with an unfamiliar prince in my own country? I could have had my own royal wedding.

That night, I sang myself to sleep with the old tunes from Oke-Odan.

James Pinson Labulo Davies
Windsor

During one of my visits to the Royal Family at their Windsor palace, Princess Alice drew me aside. She and I appeared to be about the same age, and I had always felt closest to her of all the Queen's children.

"I have something for you, Princess Sarah!" She pulled an envelope from a pocket of her large, frilly skirt and handed it to me.

"What is it do you think, Princess Alice?" We enjoyed calling each other Princess, especially because it was true.

"Why, a letter, of course," she responded with a smile. "Perhaps a secret admirer."

The Princess had recently become engaged to Prince Louis of Hesse. I believed she wished me to become engaged as well so that we could share our experiences together. However, I knew of no man who had an interest in me.

The name on the envelope read, "Captain J.P.L. Davies, retired HMRN." I pointed to the name and asked, "What is H-M-R-N?"

"Her Majesty's Royal Navy, of course!" Princess Alice replied. "I do believe it will be a proposal of marriage for you. Open it!"

Inside I found a few pieces of folded paper and a small photograph of a black man I did not immediately recognize.

"I hope this communication finds you well. You may not remember me, but you and I met at a Church Missionary Society event in Freetown hosted by your Miss Sass. I am somewhat older than you, and I do not expect you to recognize me."

I looked at the photograph again. Frequently, Miss Sass would have me attend her dinners to represent the other Female Institution students. While I could not recall him specifically, I did remember a missionary who had been travelling about Africa, promoting trade.

"He claims to have met me in Sierra Leone, Princess Alice," I said as I handed her the photograph.

"My, how handsome he is, Princess Sarah," she cooed as she studied the picture.

"Is he?" I had not yet developed a sense for what I found attractive about men. "But he is much older than we are. Should I not have someone nearer my own age?"

She giggled at my question. "Age, as you may discover, is most likely the least of your concerns about a man."

I began reading the letter once more. "Following the death of my dear wife, Matilda, I endured a proper period of mourning, but I am now endeavouring to fill that space in my life. I have been informed that you are keeping company with Her Majesty, the Queen, and her family. Upon my next visit to England, I would very much enjoy an audience with you."

I looked up and the Princess exclaimed, "Well, is it a proposal of marriage?"

After glancing at the letter once more, I responded, "I do not believe so. Perhaps you might see it differently." I handed the papers to her.

Her head bobbed up and down as she read. "My dear, he is simply smitten with you!" A broad smile appeared. "I do believe he intends to propose an engagement with you. Imagine, a captain in the Royal Navy." She gazed up slightly toward the ornate ceiling of the chamber.

He was not exactly a prince, but it was a fellow captain of the Royal Navy who had saved me from King Ghezo. "I suppose there is no harm in meeting him."

"No harm?" she echoed my words. "It shall be your destiny, my dear."

My face dropped to the floor. With the Queen's daughters marrying princes, my expectations of similar proposals deflated at the prospect of anything less.

Alice stepped up next to me and took my hand in hers. "My dear Princess Sarah." She tucked a crooked finger beneath my chin. "Believe me when I say this gentleman will probably be your bestest suitor. A young woman like yourself–from Africa, I mean– cannot expect offers of courtship from European princes, even if she is a princess herself."

The sad reality of being so different in a foreign world once again caused tears in my heart. I took great pride in my African heritage and all the cultural aspects associated with it. Even though I had spent so much of my life living with the Queen's family, these light-skinned English people still regarded me as a foreigner, someone from their inferior colonies, a social class beneath their elevated status.

A month later Mrs. Phipps summoned me to an audience with the Queen and Captain Davies. While I barely spoke, the Queen interrogated the poor soul endlessly. She inquired into his birth, his education, his service in the Royal Navy, his missionary work, his business dealings, and his proposal of marriage. Following the interview, the Queen had Captain Davies escorted out of the drawing room.

"Well, Sally, how did you find Captain Davies?" she asked.

"Your Majesty, I am relieved to hear that the good captain had the good sense to be born of Yoruba blood, like myself." The Queen smiled. "I am certain that he will make a good husband for someone, but I am not certain that person is me. Please remember I am but seventeen years."

Queen Victoria stood up from her chair and walked toward me. "Young lady, it is time for you to be settled. For most of your life, this Court has borne the cost of your living expenses, your education, and your clothing. You have wanted for nothing." She turned her face away. "Perhaps it is time for you to find your own way in this wide-ranging world. There are lessons to be learned that one cannot accomplish in the comfort of one's own home." Again, she focused her eyes upon mine. "Your Captain Davies appears to be quite willing to take you on, and it might be best for you to make use of this opportunity... while it lasts."

I turned away because I did not want her to see me weeping. The thought of leaving the Schoens saddened me, and the prospect of being married to a stranger frightened me.

"It seems obvious," she continued, "that as long as you live with that family in Gillingham, there shall be no incentive nor reason for you to marry. As a solution to this—and for your own good—we have decided that you shall remove yourself to Brighton, where you shall live with a cousin of Mrs. Phipps, a Miss Sophie Welsh."

The clouds fell on my heart and tears began to flood from my eyes. I did not want to leave the Schoens, and I did not want to marry Captain Davies. Once again, my fate had been taken from my own hands.

In Limbo
Brighton

As much as I disliked life away from the Schoens, who had become more of an adopted family to me, Brighton had a few benefits. In the mornings I could take walks along the shore and breath in the salty sea air. In some ways it reminded me a bit of Badagry. People seemed to be more jolly in Brighton. I don't ever remember hearing so much laughter and frivolity anywhere else.

One of the most disappointing aspects of life in Brighton was having to care for the older women, Miss Welsh and her widow friend Miss Barbara Simon. They asked me to accompany them on their daily outings, and I would have to walk with them and carry their various belongings, like a little slave girl. It felt like I had almost no time for my own interests.

While living with the Schoens at Palm Cottage, I had my chores, as did the rest of the family. However, most of the time I could do as I please, whether it was taking walks, studying, keeping up with my correspondence, or playing upon the piano.

Another disappointment of staying with Miss Welsh was that I was the only young person living in the home. I had no one close to my age to befriend and keep company.

Princess Alice wrote to me every week describing how Captain Davies attended the Queen in hopes of capturing my hand in marriage. It seemed the Queen would be the one to decide whom I should marry, rather than allowing me to choose for myself.

It was not that I disliked Captain Davies. I hardly knew him. Everyone else wanted to decide upon my husband, but it seemed as if there were only one choice available.

Had I remained in Africa, though, I might not have been able to choose for myself either. Most likely my parents would have selected another tribe's prince to make a political alignment and join forces. It was then I realized that my friends, Princesses Victoria and Alice, had pretty much the same arrangement.

I wrote letters to all the women I had relied upon in the past–Mrs. Forbes, Mrs. Phipps, Mrs. Schoen–asking for their guidance upon the matter of the marriage. Each of them recommended accepting Captain Davies's proposal.

Everyone seemed certain he was the proper husband—except me.

Over time, I grew weary of Brighton and Miss Welsh's house. I longed to be almost anywhere else. The only place that seemed worse would have been King Ghezo's palace in Dahomey, locked away in the dark, foul-smelling barn.

Although I possessed many skills that could have earned money, no one would hire a little black girl from Africa. I had to continue to rely upon the grace of Her Majesty for my sustenance. With no means to maintain myself, I felt trapped with Miss Welsh and her friend.

It finally occurred to me that my only escape would be to marry Captain Davies. Even though I barely knew him, it seemed worth the gamble to return to proper society and the kind of life I preferred.

Some time during your year 1861, I wrote to Queen Victoria expressing my desire to accept the proposal from Captain Davies. Everyone else in my life seemed to be very, very pleased. Not me.

Princess Alice wrote that her wedding was to be in January of the next year. We would both be eighteen years of age by then. She suggested that I marry Captain Davies about the same time so that we could arrange our weddings together. At least that provided some comfort that I could rely upon my friend as we prepared for matrimony.

Once I had made my intentions known, the Queen allowed me to return to Windsor to visit with her and the family. Captain Davies also called upon me, and we slowly learned about each other.

Although I had been present the first time Captain Davies held an audience with the Queen, she asked so many questions, and I must confess I did not listen very closely.

During our conversations I learned he had been born in Sierra Leone to Yoruba parents. Once he had completed his education in Freetown, he became a teacher at the school. Following that, he enlisted in the Royal Navy, rising to the rank of Lieutenant. At the Bombardment of Lagos, Mr. Davies became wounded and retired from the service. As part of his duties as merchant vessel captain, he visited the Female Institute in Freetown, where we met for the first time.

As the days of acquaintance passed, I began to admire Captain Davies. His commendable exploits served him well, but I could not develop an emotional attachment to him worthy of marriage. However, at that point, it felt there was no way I could refuse his hand.

121

While Alice would marry her prince at
Windsor Palace. I would be wed to
Captain Davies in Brighton at the
recently rebuilt Church of Saint
Nicholas, some 40 miles south.

The Queen's Darkest Year

Windsor

Because King Ghezo had killed my parents and the rest of the family, the unpleasant concept of death presented itself to me at an earlier age than most children. I later discovered that King Ghezo had kept me alive only to be part of a religious ritual that would have involved my own death. If not for the presence of Captain Forbes, I would not have been able to write my story for you, my friend. When the Captain died in the year of 1851, it felt as if yet another person from my own family had been taken away.

Queen Victoria herself had dealt with death all her life. Princess Alice once told me stories of her family history. Before Victoria had even been born, she had a cousin Charlotte who would have become Queen upon the death of her own father. Unfortunately, Princess Charlotte died in childbirth with no heir. Prince Edward, one of Charlotte's uncles married her husband Leopold's sister, the Princess of Saxe-Coburg-Saalfeld, and they had a daughter, Victoria. Prince Edward died when Victoria was still an infant, and she never knew her father. She became Queen in her own right upon the death of the old King, her Uncle William.

However, Queen Victoria had been told about her cousin Charlotte's difficulty with childbirth, and Victoria did not want to risk her own life bearing children. Fortunately, the good Tall Prince Albert assured her that with modern scientific methods, she would be fine and healthy.

The Queen and her Prince had many children, and I felt privileged to have known them. I could only imagine that Queen Victoria experienced the fear of losing any of her children every day.

According to Princess Alice, the Queen had never been very close to her own mother, who was known to oppose much of the politics in England. In fact, she told me that their Uncle William did not want to die before Victoria came of age for fear that her mother would act as ruler in her place. King William died one month after Victoria turned 18 years old.

Beginning in your calendar year 1861, Queen Victoria and her mother began spending more time together and patching up old wounds. In the month of March, the Queen's mother died at the age of 74 years, which was older than anyone I had ever known. Princess Alice told me the Queen grieved the loss, expressing much regret they had not been closer as family. Princess Alice had asked her mother whether we should delay our weddings, but the Queen felt the events should proceed as scheduled.

In the month of November, several cousins of the Queen and Prince Albert died. King Pedro of Portugal, and his brothers, Fernando and John, succumbed to a horrible disease called typhoid fever. The Queen continued to mourn her recently-deceased family members.

Soon after, the Tall Prince fell ill from the same disease. The Queen had held out all hope that her beloved husband would recover, but the Prince proved too weak. Within a month, the great man died as well.

Princess Alice told me that her mother continued to have a basin for shaving and a suit of clothing laid out for the Prince every day, as if he would just wake up and resume his life.

According to the English customs, people in the family of a person who died wore nothing but black clothing during a period of mourning lasting at least one year. I remember never seeing the Queen from that point on in anything but black as long as I knew her.

Following the death of Prince Albert, Queen Victoria requested Alice and me to postpone our wedding plans. She had helped me so much for so many years. I felt very badly for the Queen, and I wanted to be as respectful as possible. However, it meant that I must remain in Brighton with Miss Welsh and her friend even longer than I had hoped.

Two Weddings

Isle of Wight and Brighton

Because the Queen continued in mourning for the Tall Prince, she did not want to suffer the inconvenience of a traditional Royal Wedding. She had told Princess Alice that a chamber full of foreign dignitaries might be more than she could cope with while still grieving for her Prince.

Rather than having the ceremony at one of the main family palaces, the Queen decided to host the event at their island home, Osborne House.

During the Spring, Princess Alice would come to Brighton, and then the two of us travelled by boat to the Isle of Wight. When I first heard the name, I thought they had said, "The Isle of Whites" (or "I Love Whites") and imagined it might not be a good place for black people from Africa.

The Princess told me her mother had taken holidays there as a child. She and Prince Albert had Osborne House built as a place to escape the cold, bitter Winters. Remembering my first time in England, it was a very cold Winter, indeed.

Directly below the hill from the main house sat a private beach that only the Royal Family could use. When I looked down, I saw a strange, little carriage, and I asked the Princess what it was.

"Oh, that is Mama's bathing machine. Papa encouraged her to take the healthful benefits of sea bathing. She steps up into it and changes into her swimming costume. They roll the carriage into the water and she can simply step out the other side in total privacy. I can show it to you later, if you like!"

How strange that these English people could not just walk out into the water without some contraption to provide for their modesty. If given the opportunity, I would stride directly out into the sea on my own, given the water be sufficiently warm.

The two of us examined the sitting room and decided how the wedding party should proceed. Once the family furniture had been removed, there would be sufficient space for the event. A chamber this small could only accommodate the family and friends, as the Queen had wished.

On the day of Princess Alice's wedding, I helped her dress. So many layers of fabric. And, on top of it all, they draped a sheet of delicate lace over her that stretched from head to floor. To me, she looked like a younger version of her mother, the Queen.

The wedding party assembled in the drawing room and the ceremony commenced. I stood off to the side with the other family members, smiling for my friend. Queen Victoria wore a black dress with white trim. I could hear her sobbing beneath the black veil covering her face.

As we adjourned to the wedding breakfast, the newly-married Princess whispered to me, "You are next, Princess Sarah!"

Once I had accepted the proposal of marriage from Captain Davies, he returned to Africa to conduct his business. He had planned to return in time for our wedding date, but the death of Queen Victoria's husband caused delay.

I still knew little about the man I would soon marry. The one thing I could be sure of: he desired me to be his bride very much. He had demonstrated his devotion by petitioning the Queen over and over until I finally gave my consent. However, I kept wondering if I might have been a bad person because my reason for marrying this man were less about being in love and more about getting away from Brighton.

Princess Alice moved to Hesse, part of the German States, with her husband. The younger princesses were not quite old enough to assist me with the wedding preparations. Captain Davies sent his own sister to help me prepare for the nuptials.

While the Queen herself would not attend my wedding, as she continued in mourning, several of her staff joined me as bridesmaids. Some of Captain Davies's female relatives also participated in that capacity.

Mrs. Phipps, Mrs. Forbes, and Mrs. Schoen helped me through the day. They had all been married, and they provided the support I needed.

The weather could have been better. A light rain misted the sky. Miss Welsh brought me to St. Nicholas church in her carriage. Captain Davies's sister helped me into the white, lace-covered wedding dress, which the Queen had provided for me.

Some of the sisters helped to embellish my gown with sweet-smelling orange-blossoms. They covered my face with a lacy veil, and Captain Forbes's father, John (also a Royal Navy Captain), per-formed the act of giving me away. Captain Davies had brought with him the Lord Bishop of Sierra Leone, Edward Beckles, to officiate the ser-vice. Reverend Venn had come along to assist, and St. Nicholas's own vicar, Reverend William Nicol, who appeared to be African like me, also helped.

While Captain Davies's sisters wel-comed me into their family with the best of intentions, I could not help but think what it might have been like to have my own family with me on this special day. When the Queen's daugh-ters Victoria and Alice married, they had their family surrounding them. Thousands of miles from the land of my birth with none of my kin beside me, I felt very alone and hollow.

My head filled with cloudy images: King Ghezo's horrid palace; the first time I saw Captain Forbes and I thought he had no skin and was very powerful; meeting the Queen and wanting to run away when she touched my face and hair; how her daughters wanted to appease me by colouring one of their dolls with paint; the husband-to-be whom the Royal Family had chosen for me.

I was a gift from the King of the Blacks to the Queen of the Whites, and my life has never been one of my own choosing. Anger, fear, and grief whirled about in my head. With a room full of wedding guests, there was nowhere to run.

It would have been thrilling for me to reveal more details of the marriage service, but my mind had almost completely shut down after that. People moved their mouths, but I have no recollection of what they might have said. There is very little I can recall from the time Captain Davies appeared at the entrance with his groomsmen until the time we sat at the wedding breakfast in the lodge. I do remember large crowds and much cheering and singing.

Sometime in the late afternoon, we boarded the train for London. From there we sailed back to Freetown in Sierra Leone.

Telling you I had been a happy bride would have been my fondest wish, but I cannot impart that falsehood. Once again, I had no sense of home, and I sat next to a man I hardly knew. In my mind, I hummed the old songs from my family's village.

Mrs. Phipps later sent me a copy of the *Penny Illustrated* newspaper that had details of our wedding. The author complimented me and Captain Davies quite a bit. The article allowed me to learn more about my marriage than I had known myself.

My African Home
Freetown, Sierra Leone

Upon our return to Africa, my new husband, Captain Davies, resumed his shipping business and I went back to the Female Institution. Instead of studying, I became an instructor.

The other teachers, who were white ladies, objected to my elevation to their level. Reverend Venn, and other leaders of the Church Missionary Society, insisted I had the standing to educate other young women like myself. After all, I had been to England, spoke with the English-tongue, and had been accepted into the Queen's family.

When Miss Sass left the school a few months after I arrived, everyone thought I would be given her position. However, nature had determined a different course for me.

As Captain Davies and I got to know each other, I found him to be quite respectable and honourable. He taught me how to be a good wife, and I taught him how to be a good husband. He might not have been the kind of powerful man that my English Princess friends married, but he proved to be a wonderful companion, nonetheless.

When we received the news that I would be having a baby, I had to decline the role as headmistress. It also meant I had to leave my teaching job, which I loved very much. Every day I had the pleasure of educating young women, who frequently reminded me of myself at their age. Perhaps one of them might go on to visit the Court as I did.

The world has changed much since my childhood. Ships no longer require the wind to move, and vehicles can travel across the land without animals to pull them. Someday, perhaps in your own time, a person from my Africa will rise to become Queen or King in some other, distant land. I would like to believe that such possibilities exist.

I have chosen to write my story for you to read, my friend, while I still have time to spend as I please. I sat at my desk every day, and once I had concluded my regular correspondence, I wrote a little bit about my own life.

I wished I could have continued teaching, as I found it most fulfilling. I could only wait until I had a child of my own to raise.

Captain Davies and I have decided to name our daughter Victoria, after the woman who had supported me throughout most of my life. I wrote to the Queen to inform her of our choice.

The Queen seemed overjoyed at our naming the baby after her. She sent us a gold ceremonial tray with a small cup and cutlery to match. The inscription on the tray and cup read: "To Victoria Davies, from her godmother, Victoria, Queen of Great Britain and Ireland."

These gifts, and the gift of my child, would be something to cherish for the rest of my life. It had been an honour to have met and lived with Queen Victoria. She and her family introduced me to a life I might have never known, a life I have chosen to share with you.

And so, my friend, I conclude my story. I hope you have enjoyed learning of my days in Africa and England. Very few people ever see the range of experiences I had known, from the death of my family in Oke-Odan to my time with Queen Victoria and her children, from the isolation in King Ghezo's barn to the fulfilment of becoming a schoolteacher. I believe with all my heart that I have been truly fortunate and blessed.

From an African Princess to you, whoever you are, wherever you are, whenever you are, I bid you a good life and all the happiness you can ever find.

–Aina Sarah Forbes Bonetta Davies
Freetown, Sierra Leone, 1863

Epilogue

Sarah and Captain Davies had three children: Victoria, Arthur, and Stella. Victoria married a Nigerian doctor, John Randle, and many of their descendants are alive today. They live in England, Sierra Leone, and Nigeria.

Sarah later took ill with consumption—which we now call tuberculosis—and went to the island of Madeira to recuperate. Unfortunately, she died there 15 August 1880 and was buried at the English Cemetery in Funchal.

Captain Davies commissioned a memorial obelisk which stood in Lagos, Nigeria, with the following inscription:

IN MEMORY OF PRINCESS SARAH FORBES BONETTA

WIFE OF THE HON J.P.L. DAVIES WHO DEPARTED THIS LIFE AT MADEIRA AUGUST 15TH 1880

AGED 37 YEARS

For some historical context, the newspaper article written about the wedding between Princess Aina and Captain Davies is included in its entirety. It does not express the views of the author or the illustrator, but we thought readers might want to catch a glimpse into the world in which our heroine had lived. That it appeared in a widely-read newspaper is surprising in and of itself.

Interesting Marriage in Brighton

Penny Illustrated, August 23, 1862

On Thursday week a marriage was performed at the parish church, Brighton, to unite a lady and gentleman of colour, whose previous history gives to the ceremony a peculiar interest, thusly to those who have been so long and so deeply interested in the African race, and who have watched the progress of civilisation raised by the influence of Christianity on the negro; and the ceremony will also tell our brethren on the other side of the Atlantic that British ladies and gentlemen consider it a pleasure and a privilege to do honour to those of the African race who have proved themselves capable of appreciating the advantages of a liberal education. The lady, supposed to be an African chieftain's daughter, was presented when about the age of five year, to the late Captain Frederick Forbes, R.N., who officially visited the King of Dahomey with a view to aid the suppression of the slave trade in the interior of Africa, and in his book giving an account of the mission he thus describes the little girl: – "I have only to add a few particulars about my extraordinary present, 'the African child.'

In a former portion of these journals I have mentioned the Okeadon war. One of the captives of this dreadful slave-hunt was this interesting girl. It is usual to reserve the last born for the high behests of royalty and the immolation on the tombs of the deceased nobility. For one of these ends she had been detained at court for two years; proving by her not having been sold to the slave-traders, that she was of a good family. So extraordinary a present would have been at least a burden, had I not the conviction that, in consideration of the nature of the service I had performed, the Government would consider her as the property of the Crown. To refuse would have been to have signed her death-warrant, which, probably, would have been carried into execution forthwith. Immediately on arriving I applied, through the Secretary of the Admiralty, and received for answer that her Majesty was graciously pleased to arrange for the education and subsequent fate of the child. Of her own history she has only a confused idea. Her parents were decapitated; as to her brothers and sisters, she knows not what their fate might have been. For her age, supposed to be eight years, she is a perfect genius. She now speaks English well, and has a great talent for music. She has won the affections, with but few exceptions, of all who have known her by her decent and amiable conduct, which nothing can exceed. She is far in advance of any white child of her age in aptness of learning, and

strength of mind and affection; and with her, being an excellent specimen of the negro race, might be tested the capability mindset of the black, it being generally and commonly supposed that after a certain age the intellect becomes impaired and the pursuit of knowledge impossible; that, though the negro child may be clever, the adult will be dull and stupid. Her head is considered so excellent a phrenological specimen, and illustrating such high intelligence, that M. Pistrucci, the medallist to the Mint, has undertaken to make a bust of her, intending to present a cast to the author. Her mind has received a moral and religious impression, and she was baptised, according to the rites of the Protestant Church, Sarah Forbes Bonetta." Her Majesty provided the means for completing the education of Miss Sarah Forbes Bonetta, whose knowledge and accomplishments now make her an ornament for any society, and prove most satisfactorily that the African mind is capable of the highest intellectual attainments. Her Majesty has taken a great interest in her marriage, and given it her full sanction. At the same time she has, besides presents from the Royal family, herself provided the whole of the outfit, &c. Mr. James Davis, the bridegroom, was originally a slave taken by one of our cruisers, and educated in the schools of the Church Missionary Society at Sierra Leone; and, showing himself to possess great talents and capable of profiting by education, was, with the sanction, of the

Admiralty, placed in an official capacity upon one of her Majesty's ships, under the care of Captain Coote, R.N., and proved himself so useful and willing as to gain the good wishes and opinions of both officers and men. He afterwards commenced trading on his own account, and is now a prosperous and influential merchant at Lagos, employing upwards of a hundred of his fellow-countrymen and trying to improve their moral and intellectual status.

As early as ten o'clock on the morning of the marriage the approaches to the Old Church, by way of Church-street, North-street, and Church-hill, were thronged with crowds of persons anxiously waiting for the opening of the church doors. Before that time a large number of ladies, provided with tickets, were admitted by the north-east entrance, and took up the best position they could near the altar. About half-past ten a "couple" presented themselves at the hymeneal altar to be made one. The reverend vicar performed the ceremony, which had scarcely concluded when the first carriage of *the party* arrived at the northern entrance. All eyes instantly left the newly-married couple, and were directed to the vestry door. Here entered four bridemaids–ladies of colour–apparelled in white dresses, with red ribbon trimming extending round the neck and across the chest; a broad sash of the same coloured material being fastened round the waist, long streaming ends reaching almost to the

ground, white tarlatan opera-cloaks were thrown over their shoulders, and the heads were encircled with bonnets of tulle of the purest white and of the latest fashion, the caps being formed of blonde interspersed with apple-blossom. In these all interest was centred, until a few minutes later four fair bridemaids entered the sacred edifice, two of them were attired similar to their sister (African) bridemaids, whilst the other two wore "forget-me-nots" in their bonnets; and their white bonnets were trimmed with blue ribbon, with sashes to match. The next party that arrived included the bridegroom and five coloured groomsmen. Then followed six fair young ladies, varying from about twelve to six years of age, also bridemaids. These, too, were also dressed in white, with white Tuscan hats trimmed–two with apple-blossoms and four with "forget-me-nots," with white lace streamers hanging tastefully down their backs. Four English bridegrooms and one coloured gentleman concluded the party, with the exception of the numerous friends. The excitement then became intense–all that was wanting was the bride. Some few minutes elapsed, all eyes being riveted on the door. At length a cheer and clapping of hands from the hundreds without the building announced her arrival. Steadfastly was she scanned from head to foot. She was robed in pure white. Her dress was of glacé silk, the trimmings being of the same material. A wreath of orange-blossoms encircled her brow, and a veil of white lace hung tastefully from it over her shoulders and bosom. She was met at the door by the bridegroom, and appeared considerably nervous, the innocent throbbing of her breast being very perceptible through her transparent wedding-garments. Of her personal qualities we may safely say she is one of the prettiest coloured ladies we ever beheld. There is a distinct absence of that abruptness in the features so often seen in the females of the African race, which gives them an air of ferocity. She has an eye expressive of tenderness and beaming with intelligence, whilst her whole deportment is ladylike in the extreme. On the arrival of the bride all was in readiness. The bridal party was ranged before the altar. Next behind the bride and bridegroom stood the children, then the African and English bridemaids, mingled in pleasing confusion, whilst the groomsmen brought up the rear. The entire length of the nave of the church was crammed with people, anxious to obtain a glimpse of the ceremony. The Right Rev. the Lord Bishop of Sierra Leone, assisted by the Rev. Henry Venn and the Rev. William Nicol—a gentleman of colour—performed the service, which was strictly in accordance with the form of the Church of England. Immediately on the reverend Bishop commencing the prayers the utmost silence prevailed, but the responses were uttered in so low a tone by the bride and bridegroom that they were perfectly inaudible even at but a few yards from the altar. Captain Forbes, R.N., father of the late Captain Forbes, who brought Miss Bonetta to England, gave away the bride, The ceremony lasted about three-quarters of an hour, when, the registry having been signed, the happy couple and the bridal party left the church, being lustily cheered on their exit by the populace, which had assembled in hundreds at the vestry door. A merry peal on the church bells added much of the cheerfulness of the scene at the conclusion of the ceremony.

A breakfast on a splendid scale, served up in the garden of West Hill Lodge, followed, which was partaken of by a large and distinguished company, including the newly-married couple, the Bishop of Sierra Leone, Captain Forbes, several clergymen connected with the district and the Church Missionary Society, and a number of ladies. The Rev. H. Venn proposed the health of the "Bride and Bridegroom," to which the bridegroom replied, and in doing so expressed himself highly indebted to Englishmen for their kindness since he had been among them. The proceedings were brought to a conclusion about half-past four by the singing of the "Doxology," and the happy pair left for London, and it is said they intend starting shortly for Sierra Leone, and expect to be there in about a month.

About the Author

WAYNE GOODMAN has lived in the San Francisco Bay Area most of his life (with too many cats). When not writing, he enjoys playing Gilded Age parlour music on the piano, with an emphasis on women, gay, and black composers.

About the Illustrator

AJUAN MANCE is a Professor of English and Ethnic Studies at Mills College and a lifelong artist and writer. Ajuan has participated in solo and group exhibitions as well as comic and zine fests, from the Bay Area to Brooklyn.

Lightning Source UK Ltd.
Milton Keynes UK
UKHW051037221220
375528UK00006B/91